ROAD TRANSPORT GWENT
by Paul Heaton

P.M. Heaton Publishing
Abergavenny, Monmouthshire
Great Britain
2004

Front Cover: It was rare to see J.M. Watkins' entire fleet together. This view at Westgate Garage, Llanfoist, in the shadow of the Blorenge Mountain, shows that by 1976 he had standardised on the ERF tractor unit.

Title Page: A Leyland Octopus 8 wheeled rigid, GDW 930 belonging to British Road Services and driven by Larry Petit seen on its side after a road accident at Jayne's Pitch, Brynmawr. Operating from the BRS Cwm Depot the vehicle was carrying steel coils from Richard Thomas & Baldwin's Ebbw Vale Works. Before the advent of coil wells it was carried on flatbed lorries, such as illustrated, with timber battens making a temporary channel for the load. Seen on the lorry is Colin Addis with the Cwm Depot Manager, Jack Matthews looking on.

Back Cover: A gleaming unit of Harry Morgan's fleet, an ERF, shown in 2003.

ISBN 1 872006 17 5

© First Edition October, 2004

Published by P.M. Heaton Publishing,
Abergavenny, Monmouthshire, NP7 8NG

Printed in Great Britain by
The Amadeus Press Ltd.,
Cleckheaton, West Yorkshire, BD19 4TQ

Typeset by Highlight Type Bureau, Bradford BD8 7BY

CONTENTS

PREFACE

This volume is to be the first in a series of photographic records dealing with road transport in South Wales and the Border Country. For this book I have featured firms operating in Gwent, or more correctly, the old County of Monmouthshire. Included are fleets involved in a wide range of activities, from tippers to steel haulage, furniture removals, livestock transport and heavy haulage.

The industrial valleys of Monmouthshire were home to considerable industrial developments, coal mines of which there were dozens – alas none of which survive today, steel plants, and even a glass works, and in the main it is the transport businesses which served these which are included.

I am most grateful to all those who have kindly helped with photographs and information, including Tim Barry, Roy Caswell, Brian Edwards, the late John Emery, the late David Evans, Richard Evans, John Fletcher, Howard Francis, David Hughes, Brian Jowitt, Mike Kelly, Roy Fox, the late Cyril Lane, Vernon Lane, Jack Matthews, John Meredith, Gary Morgan, Roger Morgan, Alan Sadler, John Watkins, William Watkins, R.A. Whitehead and Cyril Williams.

To anyone else who has helped – thank you. To the reader, I hope you enjoy the book – in many ways a look back in time.

Paul Heaton
Abergavenny
October, 2004

Emlyn Evans & Son, Pontypool acquired this Gardner-engined ERF 6wl twin-steer dropside lorry RWO93 new in 1957. It is shown at GKN Cwmbran loaded with engine blocks destined for Perkins at Peterborough.

ISAAC CASWELL, EBBW VALE

One of the most important names in road haulage in the old County of Monmouth was that of 'Caswell'. Isaac Caswell had been a miner at Cwm Colliery, near Ebbw Vale, and in 1890 having identified the opportunities in road haulage, set himself up in business as a carrier with a single horse and cart. Early work involved hauling miner's coal from Cwm, Waunllwyd and Ebbw Vale Collieries, and in the summer months this was supplemented with hauling chippings for use when the roads were being tarred. Business expanded and by the 1920s upwards of twenty horses and carts were in use.

In the early 1920s they acquired their first petrol-engined vehicle, which was one of the first two tippers operated in the area. Based on a Dennis chassis it was fitted with three pit drams, one on each side with a third at the rear, all independently operated. This investment was followed by substantial expansion, and apart from the transport of coal, chippings, etc., Isaac became involved with the haulage of steel from the giant Ebbw Vale Steelworks.

Of Isaac's four sons three joined him in the business, whilst Walter set out on his own, operating tippers and trading as Walter Caswell Coal Haulage. Brothers Bert, Isaac junior and Harry continued to expand the original business which now traded as Isaac Caswell and Sons, later simply as I. Caswell and Sons, from premises at Pennant Street, Ebbw Vale.

In 1947 Isaac Caswell (the son) established another business which traded as I. Caswell (Ebbw Vale) Ltd and was almost entirely involved with the carriage of steel from Ebbw Vale. He remained as a partner in the original business with his brothers Bert and Harry, and both firms continued to share the same premises at Pennant Street, and outwardly most would not have realised that there were two businesses – a partnership and a limited company.

After the Second World War I. Caswell (Ebbw Vale) Ltd acquired its first 8 wheeler, a Thornycroft, one of only five of this model operating in Monmouthshire at that time. Both fleets shared the same livery – blue with red wheels and chassis with white lettering, and whilst the company tended to operate larger vehicles on longer distance work the partnership used smaller lorries usually on more localised work and internally within the steelworks.

Isaac was joined in I. Caswell (Ebbw Vale) Ltd by his three eldest sons, Graham, John and Roy, and with the death of his brother Bert, Harry was eventually joined in I. Caswell and Sons by Isaac's fourth son Gwyn.

In 1962 it was found that the two businesses had outgrown the Pennant Street premises at Ebbw Vale and as a result whilst the partnership remained there, the company moved to newly acquired premises at Llanfoist Sawmills near Abergavenny. This location was particularly suitable for the long distance operations being situated just off the Heads of the Valleys Road.

In the late 1940s with the threat of nationalisation hanging over their heads, it was decided to dispose of the Thornycroft 8 wheeler. This was done because Isaac knew that hauliers were losing their vehicles and having to wait long periods for compensation. He sensibly decided that if the vehicle was going, better to be paid promptly for it.

In the event neither firm was nationalised, because at that time both managed to show that a high percentage of their work was localised. During this period they managed to operate on permits up to twenty-five miles, which covered Newport Docks and at a stretch as far as Swansea.

Isaac having sold his Thornycroft 8 wheeler, then went out and bought more. These were subsequently replaced in the early 1950s by seven Atkinson's – three on 'A' licence and four on contract to and in the colours of Richard Thomas and Baldwin Ltd., Ebbw Vale. In the early 1960s these were traded into Praill's of Hereford, the contract vehicles were replaced with Foden 8 wheelers, whilst the 'A' licence vehicles were replaced by a fleet of seven Albion 6 wheelers, a model which was particularly suitable for economic loads of steel and were fitted with coil wells. The partnership in Ebbw Vale also operated two of this model.

In 1965 Caswell's started to convert their fleets to articulated outfits. Originally selecting tried and tested makes such as ERF, Atkinson, Seddon, Guy and Foden with 150 Gardner engines and later the 180, they then tried Volvo F86 and F88 models and subsequently Bedford for lighter work and Mercedes for heavier distance operations.

With the death of brother Graham in 1963 and the retirement of John in 1984 Roy Caswell was joined by his wife Phyllis and they continued to operate the expanded fleet of I. Caswell (Ebbw Vale) Ltd with 28 tractor units and 57 semi-trailers. A new firm was started called Llanfoist Light Haulage and nine smaller vehicles and vans were operated. Brother Gwyn eventually changed the partnership title and henceforth operated as D.G. Caswell Haulage Ltd.

With the contraction of Ebbw Vale Steelworks the company diversified into other fields and new customers included Crown Cork of Tredegar, OP Chocolate of Merthyr Tydfil, and other work included exhaust systems for Vauxhall cars and car seat cushions.

The business celebrated its centenary in 1990, but within a few years Roy Caswell and his wife decided to retire and the vehicles were sold off. Thus an important chapter in road haulage which had operated for over a hundred years had, sadly, come to an end.

Overleaf: Isaac Caswell taking delivery of the first of seven Albion Reiver 6 wheelers WCJ301 from Ted Praill.

Opposite top:
This Thornycroft acquired new in the late 1940s was Caswell's first 8 wheeler.

Opposite bottom:
LVJ77 was one of seven Gardner-engined Atkinson 8 wheelers bought new from Praills of Hereford in the early 1950s. Three operated on 'A' licences whilst four were on contract to and in the colours of Richard Thomas & Baldwin Ltd., Ebbw Vale. This particular vehicle was later traded into Praills around 1960 who operated it as a tar tanker on contract to Berry Wiggins for over a further decade. Roy Caswell was the driver when photographed.

Above:
One of four Foden 8 wheelers which I. Caswell (Ebbw Vale) Ltd had on contract to Richard Thomas & Baldwin., Ebbw Vale, from 1960.

Photographed in front of this Guy Invincible articulated outfit are *from left* Max Gill, Bert Smith, Bill Bowyer, Phillip Caswell (Graham's son), Clive Bates, Isaac Caswell, Jim Gill and Roy Caswell.

By 1968 I. Caswell (Ebbw Vale) Ltd were operating ten articulated tractor units, including Volvo, Seddon, Foden, ERF, Atkinson and Guy. This photograph was taken at their Llanfoist Sawmill yard.

A pair of Cummins-engined Atkinson Borderer tractor units, HAX393L and CWO836K shown at Llanfoist.

Seddon-Atkinson YTX761T shown delivering seating for the grandstand at an Irish Golf Tournament.

Driver Ron Williams with a 1979 Seddon-Atkinson unit BAX129T.

Two Seddon-Atkinson tractor units, FAX128V and D959NHB dating from 1980 and 1987 respectively.

Bedfords were eventually adopted for lighter work. This TM tractor unit is seen coupled to a box-van semi trailer (B955UBM).

E.R. CLISSOLD, ABERGAVENNY

Ernest Richard Clissold entered business as a haulage contractor at Abergavenny around 1936, and apart from specialising in livestock transport and timber extraction, moved into household removals with the purchase of the old established firm of John Ross. Originally operating from premises at Hatherleigh Road, Abergavenny, after the war he gradually concentrated on general haulage. He avoided nationalisation in the late 1940s due to the majority of his work being local.

In the period from 1950 he owned four wheelers, mostly Commers which were usually used for the carriage of agricultural produce and fertilizers. With his death the business passed to his daughter Elsie Summers and her family. By 1966 two articulated outfits and a 4 wheel Commer were being operated, and the majority of work undertaken was the carriage of steel from Llanwern steelworks. Long time drivers of E.R. Clissold were Ken Edwards and his son Brian.

In 1967 Cyril Lane of W.G. Lane and Sons, Garage Proprietors and Coach Operators of Abergavenny and Llanvetherine, became aware that the business was on the market, and bought the Commer 4 wheeler which he used on a night and day service carrying steel from Llanwern, with Ken and Brian Edwards driving.

Cyril Lane, himself from an old established local business, used the Commer to generate the capital to purchase his first articulated lorry, a Guy Big 'J', NWO510F, which was fitted with a Gardner 180 engine. This vehicle was used alongside the Commer, again on night and day operation, and subsequently another Guy was purchased, this being OWO282F. When a third Guy tractor unit arrived the Commer was sold.

Eventually the fleet operated under the name of E.R. Clissold numbered ten tractor units with substantially more trailers. Subsequently they were to be found employed on hauling containers from Bellferry, and later from British Steel at Ebbw Vale.

Volvo and Ford Transcontinental tractor units have been operated followed by Seddon-Atkinson 4x2 and 6x2 vehicles. With the general contraction in the steel industry in South Wales, whilst many haulage businesses have disappeared, E.R. Clissold have contracted to take account of this, and Brian Edwards is still driving for them.

Sadly, Cyril Lane passed away in 2001, but the various businesses which make up W.G. Lane and Sons continue to thrive under the direction of his widow Rita, and their children Vernon and Janet with a loyal long serving group of staff.

Whilst Lane's operate garage premises at Llanvetherine and Lion Street, Abergavenny, the commercial end of the operation is based on their Mill Street, Abergavenny premises.

Currently a large fleet of coaches is being operated and a big fleet of breakdown vehicles. In fact W.G. Lane and Sons are the largest recovery service operating in the North of Gwent, but serving a far wider area with their level of expertise.

FLEET LIST

Index No.	Fleet No.	Vehicle	Date Aqd.	
–		Commer 4wl flat	1967	
NWO510F	1	Guy Big 'J' articulated	1967	
OWO282F	2	Guy Big 'J' articulated	1968	
RAX560G	3	Guy Big 'J' articulated	1968	
TAX222G	4	Guy Big 'J' articulated	1969	
UWO140H	5	Guy Big 'J' articulated	1969	
WWO182J	6	Guy Big 'J' articulated	1970	
XWO200J	7	Guy Big 'J' articulated	1970	
AAX368J	8	Atkinson Borderer articulated	1971	
	9	Atkinson Borderer articulated	1971	
JEU25J	10	Seddon 4wl flat	1972	New in 1970 to Cyril Williams, Brynmawr.
	11			

KAX411L	12	Atkinson Borderer articulated
	13	
	14	
	15	
PWC502R	16	Volvo F88 articulated
NFO580R	17	Seddon Atkinson articulated
SRJ800R	18	Ford Transcontinental articulated
UAX310S	19	Ford Transcontinental articulated
YDJ694T	20	Ford Transcontinental articulated
MJN713V	21	Ford Transcontinental articulated
WPU569W	22	Seddon Atkinson articulated
SDM680V	23	Ford Transcontinental articulated
B827BNY	24	Volvo F12 articulated
XAL800Y	25	Ford Transcontinental articulated
GTW715Y	26	Ford Transcontinental articulated
D564OOB	27	Volvo FL10 articulated
D575OOB	28	Volvo FL10 articulated
B441SNB	29	Volvo F7 articulated
F443BOP	30	Volvo FL10 articulated
D756BOP	31	Volvo FL10 articulated
H128OKG	32	Volvo FL10 articulated
A694JFA	33	Volvo F12 articulated
H36VFO	34	Volvo FL10 articulated
P264VEU	35	Seddon Atkinson articulated
X384CDW	36	Seddon Atkinson articulated

Left:
A young Ken Edwards driving an E.R. Clissold lorry at Abergavenny Carnival.

Opposite top:
Pictured with this 1955 Commer 4 wheeler NAX772 in Mountjoy Street, Abergavenny, are Dick Clissold (left) and driver Ken Edwards.

Opposite bottom:
Following the acquisition of the E.R. Clissold business by W.G. Lane & Sons the fleet was built up until by 1968 three Guy Big 'J' articulated tractor units were owned. They were NWO510F (1), OWO282F (2) and RAX560G (3).

Above:
Ken Edwards is pictured outside the Mill Street, Abergavenny premises of W.G. Lane & Sons, with Volvo F88 tractor unit PWC502R (16).

Opposite top: Volvo F88 PWC502R (16) and Atkinson Borderer KAX411L (12).

Opposite bottom: Volvo F12 B827BNY (24).

19

Opposite top:
This Foden breakdown vehicle 83HHO is photographed with Abergavenny Castle in the background.

Opposite bottom:
Pictured at the Mill Street, Abergavenny premises of W.G. Lane & Sons, is a small part of the breakdown fleet. Lanes'are the biggest recovery operator in the North of Gwent, but their expertise and operation extends over a far wider area.

Above:
W.G. Lane & Sons operate a large fleet of coaches.

DAVIES & MEREDITH, BRYNMAWR

The Brynmawr haulage business of Davies & Meredith Ltd was founded in 1947 by Leonard Llewellyn Davies and Jack Meredith when they acquired a former U.S. Army Studbaker 6 wheel flat lorry which was used on local work. They quickly obtained regular work carrying a special limestone for use in the making of bricks from a quarry in the Hafod on the Blackrock to North Wales, and further expansion was found using tippers at local quarries.

In the 1950s with the opening of the Dunlop Semtex Factory at Brynmawr a contract was obtained to carry their products, and this arrangement lasted until the closure of the plant in 1981.

With their involvement with Dunlop Semtex this called for much flat work, and the eventual conversion to articulation. Always fans of the Atkinson 8 wheeler with a Gardner 150 engine, two of these in tipper form spent many years in the fleet, specifically JEU376 and HEU799, which were subsequently converted to flats, and finally into 4x2 articulated tractor units. In the 1960s Bedford 'S' type 4 wheel rigids and later Bedford TKs were used, and from 1967 articulated tractors of this make coupled to 4 in line trailers. For a period an amalgamation was effected with the other main carrier at Dunlop Semtex, that being Lewis Owen's Black Rock Haulage Co. Ltd., but this arrangement was eventually disbanded.

Len Davies died in 1990 and Jack Meredith's son John had been involved in the business for fourteen years prior. Whilst ERF and other makes have been used Davies & Meredith have always turned back to the Atkinson and later Seddon Atkinson vehicle. Whilst Gardner engined vehicles predominated early on, as the country's motorway network developed with higher sustained speed, the Cummins engine was adopted as standard.

With their distinctive red livery, until quite recently there were around sixteen tractor units with 30 trailers involved in general haulage, but normally employed carrying steel tubes and steel coils and plate mainly on long distance work. However with the closure of Ebbw Vale Steelworks and the contraction of industry generally in the area it was no surprise to see the passing of yet another old established and respected transport business.

Pictured in front of this Atkinson 8 wheel tipper JEU376 are Jack Meredith (left) and driver Albert Waters from Brynmawr. Supplied new in 1958 by Coventry & Jeffs, Bristol, the vehicle was fitted with a Gardner 150 engine.

Two Seddon tractor units PEU598N and PEU597N which were bought new in 1974. The latter vehicle was the first Davies & Meredith vehicle to be fitted with a Cummins 220 engine. By day it delivered a load of steel to the Midlands as well as a local delivery, and by night trunked a load to Shepherds Bush, London, where two other vehicles were based by the firm. In all the vehicle covered 500/600 miles a day, and ran for eight years on the original engine, which was the reason that Davies & Meredith changed to Cummins.

Co-founder Len Davies is seen in May 1980 with this new ERF 'B' series 4x2 tractor unit.

A general view of the Brynmawr yard of Davies & Meredith Ltd. A Seddon-Atkinson tractor unit is shown with a host of trailers.

An ERF E320 6x2 tractor unit and trailer D680NUH is shown in Intermediate Road, Brynmawr with a school portokabin which was carried from Cardiff.

Workshop staff seen in front of an ERF twin steer tractor unit. From left: Sid Page, Alan Way and Royston Burgoyne.

RWO93	ERF 6wl twin-steer 12ton dropside	1957	
SWO800	AEC Mustang 6wl twin-steer 12ton dropside	1958	
UWO774	BMC 8ton flat	1959	
VWO596	Leyland Super Comet 9ton dropside	1959	
WAX740	Commer 6wl 10ton dropside	1959	
505BLV	Commer 6wl 10ton flat	1959	New in 1959, bought secondhand
WWO284	Commer 6wl 10ton flat	1959	
WWO741	Commer 7 ton dropside	1959	
219AAX	Commer 7ton dropside	1960	
226BAX	Commer 6wl 10ton flat	1961	

Above:
Emlyn Evans employed a number of drivers who lived in Usk. As a result arrangements were made for their vehicles to be parked overnight at the rear of Vivien Etheridge's Woodside Garage. Unfortunately Usk was prone to flooding and this happened on December 1, 1960. As a result it was decided that the Gardner-engined ERF twin-steer dropside RWO93 would tow the Commer dropside WWO741 out of the flooded area before starting its engine. The photograph shows this taking place. The reproduction is poor as it is taken from the South Wales Argus of that date.

Overleaf:
Emlyn Evans' pride and joy was this Maudslay 8 wheeler HAX350 which he bought new in 1949. The vehicle's headboard reflected his main customer – Partridge Jones & John Paton Ltd. of Pontnewynydd Forge. Alas later that year it went to British Road Services when his fleet was nationalised.

Seen at the GKN Factory at Cwmbran this ERF 6wl twin-steer dropside lorry RWO93 is loaded with engine blocks for Perkins at Peterborough.

EVANS TRANSPORT, TREDEGAR

David Thomas Evans, the founder of Evans Transport was born in 1914 and was a native of Tredegar. He was in fact one of four brothers all being musicians who played in a dance band as 'Elwyn Evans and his Dance Orchestra'. Elwyn being his elder brother.

David's brother-in-law, Horace Stephens, was the buyer for Whitehead's Steel, and he introduced him to their Transport Manager, a Mr. Basden, which resulted in David obtaining a contract for two vehicles (one then and one to follow) to transport steel from Whitehead's Newport plant mainly to the Midlands. David had already acquired an ex-Military Canadian Chevrolet 6 wheeled dropside lorry, which apart from being bonneted had left hand drive. Eventually he ran two Dennis 4 wheelers on this work.

After two years, in 1948 he was awarded a further contract, this time with Lysachts of Newport to run 800 tons of steel coil per week from the Ebbw Vale works of Richard Thomas and Baldwin to Lysachts Corporation Road, Newport works. He had at first to convince the Transport Manager at Lysachts, Bill Clissold, that he could carry out this contract. It was something of a new innovation to transport steel in coils, and Lysachts were aware that if consigned to the railway continuous production would be difficult to achieve at their end. David Evans proposed a schedule involving two eight wheelers running round the clock employing four drivers in total, and this was found to be acceptable. As a result of this contract he entered into partnership with his father and brother Elwyn, and all three of their names appeared on the carriers licences. They then obtained two Thornycroft 8 wheel flats new from Praills of Hereford, the first was GWO184 costing £3,100 and the second GWO226 costing £3,300.

In 1949 with the nationalisation of road haulage, whilst British Road Services took their work they did not take the Evans vehicles. In effect they still owned the lorries, but had virtually no work for them. They did manage to get one days work per week and eventually a little more on permit. With the Midlands clamouring for steel it wasn't long before they were running two loads a day, but this was mainly due to the good offices of Lysachts.

Thereafter he obtained work for large capacity tippers carrying coal and coke, and initially obtained an AEC Mk3 Mammoth Major HZ5640 which had a wooden drop side body. This vehicle which had originally been built for export had a 11.3 engine and was one of only two believed to be operated in the United Kingdom. Originally owned in Ireland, death duties had apparently forced its sale, and David Evans obtained it through Tom Bird of Stratford on Avon.

Eventually David's father and brother decided to withdraw from the business, and to achieve this the vehicles were sold off but it wasn't long before he was back in business having bought back some of the original vehicles.

Subsequently he was running a small fleet of 8 wheeled tippers, and the steel transport was eventually carried on a newly acquired fleet of articulated vehicles. Evans Transport ran AEC, Seddon and Guy tractor units, but eventually standardised on Volvo.

In the late 1980s the vehicles were disposed of and yet another well known name in the haulage industry had disappeared from the scene.

Left:
Part of the fleet of tractor units operated in the late 1960s, including Seddon, AEC Mandator and Volvo F86 and F88 units.

Overleaf:
This AEC Mammoth Major Mk 3 dropside tipper HZ5640 started life in Ireland, but was used on an important coal and coke contract. Unusually it was fitted with the AEC 11.3 engine hence the radiator protruded further than is normal for this model.

PHONE
2141

EVANS TRANSPORT
TREDEGAR

HZ 5640

This AEC Mammoth Major Mk5 tipper was delivered new by Praills of Hereford.

Left:
Bedford pantechnicon CDJ136T dating from 1978 was normally used on household removals.

Below:
This Scania 92m drawbar outfit E360GLK in the Pantechnicon green livery was one of three operating a regular removal service to and from France and Spain. International Household Removals are an important part of the firm's business.

RICHARD MARSTON, PONTYPOOL

Richard Marston entered road haulage in the early 1960s carrying mainly agricultural goods and was based at a yard on the Brecon Road, Abergavenny. He had earlier had an involvement with plant, and for a time was involved with both. After a few years he moved his operating base to the Old Workhouse in Abergavenny, and soon started hauling for the nearby Abergavenny Concrete Company of Union Road. He soon consolidated his business by buying Abergavenny Concrete's two Dodge drop side tippers, making him their sole carrier.

He continued to operate mostly on restricted 'B' licences until in 1969 he obtained his first 'A' licence and purchased his first articulated outfit. Bought new from Praills (Hereford) Ltd., this was a Perkins engined Seddon tractor unit with a tandem axled coil trailer – UAX142H. His principal work with this vehicle was out of Richard Thomas and Baldwin's Ebbw Vale Works, and the vehicle was finished in his early livery of green and red.

With the closure of the Brecon Road Railway sidings at Abergavenny he spread his vehicles from his nearby yard over this area. A period of rapid expansion took place and he was soon operating around a dozen tractor units with a host of trailers, and also undertook some low loader work. Some of the earlier vehicles were ERF, Atkinson, Seddon and eventually Daf.

Subsequently he moved his business to the Polo Grounds at New Inn, Pontypool, having acquired the former premises of West Mon. Motors. Expansion continued, and he took over the transport for Henley Fork Lift Trucks at Pontllanfraith. This work involved the purchase of Henley's own fleet of tractor units, mostly based on Scania and their specialist trailers. Because Henley's colours were yellow with red lettering, these colours were thereafter adopted by Richard Marston for his whole fleet.

Apart from work for Henleys he carried out low loader movements for the Dowlais Foundry near Merthyr Tydfil and had a substantial number of vehicles operating on steel transport from the Ebbw Vale and Llanwern steelworks.

From one of the smallest operators in the 1960s he became one of the largest haulage contractors in the area by 1980. However thereafter he decided to withdraw from haulage altogether, and concentrated on farming, clearly believing that it was a better and more stable investment. Motor vehicles depreciate, property and land do not.

This DAF articulated outfit CHB208V shown in Cross Street, Abergavenny, was one of a large number of this make operated by Richard Marston Ltd in the late 1970s and early 1980s.

This Cummins-engine ERF tractor unit YBO662T is seen passing the Swan Hotel, Abergavenny, whilst participating in the Abergavenny Carnival.

Used mainly on steel traffic this ERF, WTG912T was painted in the later yellow and red livery.

H. MORGAN & SONS, CWM

Harry Morgan entered business as a coal merchant and haulage contractor at Cwm, Ebbw Vale, in 1945. His father-in-law traded as E.W. Alford at Cwm as a coal merchant, and it was no surprise when Harry started up on his own. Early work included the delivery of miner's coal in the area from the Marine Colliery at Cwm. Initially he operated from the rear of his home at 12, Ash Street, Cwm, but later obtained premises at Newcombe Terrace.

In the mid-1950s, whilst continuing as a coal merchant and still delivering miner's coal, he entered steel haulage by acquiring two 4 wheel rigids with their 'A' licences, one of these being a Praills of Hereford manufactured Proctor, which were built in the postwar period. Both were quickly replaced with BMC 7ton 4wheel rigid flats, NBO89 and LKG533, which were bought new from City Motors, Cardiff.

Whilst expansion continued at a moderate pace, in 1959 they purchased a Thames Trader 4x2 tractor unit with a single axle 4 in line semi trailer, and this vehicle held the distinction of being the first articulated outfit to work out of Ebbw Vale Steelworks. This was soon replaced by a Bedford 'S' type.

Although articulation became the name of the game in road haulage, they also continued to operate 4 and 6 wheeled rigids, including two Albion Reivers which came from Parfitts of Ebbw Vale together with their carriers licences. This pair, VVJ123 and VVJ294 were soon painted out in Harry Morgan's green livery.

Harry Morgan was joined in the business by his sons Roger and Anthony, and eventually with the closure of the British Road Services depot at Marine Street, Cwm, in 1975 they acquired these premises, which remain as the firm's operating base.

Gradually the coal round was disposed of, and expansion saw the business operating upwards of a dozen tractor units with twice as many trailers.

With the death of Harry, his two sons carried on the business and were joined by their own sons, Richard and Gary, but in 1989 Anthony retired. In 1995 they proudly celebrated 50 years in haulage.

With the closure of Ebbw Vale Steelworks and the Aberbeeg Brewery, two of their major customers, much of their traditional work had disappeared. However, they have managed to find new work, particularly transporting timber products, and are currently operating six articulated tractor units and two 4-wheeled rigid flats.

A rare survivor.

Two long serving drivers are of note. Les Cross recently retired at 67 having originally started as a 15 year old with Harry Morgan's father-in-law E.W. Alford, and following army service was continuously employed by the firm until his retirement. Idris Rawle has worked for the firm for 51 years from 15 years of age on their coal round and has driven for them since he was old enough. He has never had any other employer, and is still with the firm. You cannot buy loyalty.

FLEET LIST

Index No.	Make & Type
DTR961	Bedford tipper
DFH501	Bedford tipper
DBK909	Bedford tipper
HYD168	Bedford tipper
HUH222	Bedford tipper
ECJ51	Austin 4wl flat
	Austin 4wl flat
FVJ836	Proctor 4wl flat
LKG533	BMC 4wl flat
NBO89	BMC 4wl flat

OAX739	BMC 4wl flat
OAX740	BMC 4wl flat
PBO725	BMC 4wl flat
SUH827	BMC 4wl flat
UAX21	Thames Trader articulated
UAX375	BMC 4wl flat
VVJ123	Albion 6wl flat
VVJ294	Albion 6wl flat
YAX841	Bedford 'S' type articulated
512FWO	Albion articulated
527GAX	Albion articulated
743GWO	Albion articulated
932HWO	Dodge 4wl flat
AAX67B	Dodge articulated
BAX---B	Dodge articulated
EAX981C	Leyland articulated
BDE901C	Leyland articulated
LAX301E	Dodge articulated
LAX302E	Dodge articulated
NAX554F	Ford articulated
NWO510F	Guy Big 'J' articulated
VWO634H	Leyland Beaver articulated
XAX435J	Seddon articulated
BTG449J	Atkinson articulated
AWO902K	Atkinson articulated
EWO769L	Atkinson articulated
LHB252P	Daf articulated
WKG448T	Daf articulated
GTG739T	Daf articulated
GTG740T	Daf articulated
UUH663S	ERF articulated
XHB745T	ERF articulated
LUH493X	Daf articulated
KAX841W	Daf articulated

B459ATH	Daf articulated
D262OVW	Daf articulated
RDW551T	Daf articulated
A257VNY	Daf articulated
B205DGC	Daf articulated
B459ATH	Daf articulated
C339KGT	Leyland articulated
C259ERO	Leyland articulated
D262OVW	Daf articulated
E------	Daf articulated
E554PUB	Leyland articulated
E829BBW	Leyland articulated
E395SWD	ERF articulated
E---OWT	Foden articulated
E616FJM	Leyland Daf articulated
E806UKG	ERF articulated
E101TDW	ERF articulated
F485OTC	Leyland articulated
G906HLH	Foden articulated
J323ETU	Foden articulated
J324ETU	Foden articulated
J---BNW	Foden articulated
J143OEW	ERF articulated
J904TOF	ERF articulated
L78UFL	ERF articulated
L755KFU	ERF articulated
M647XFM	ERF articulated
M213CAE	Iveco 4wl flat
J610RK	Leyland 4wl flat
N827OEG	ERF articulated
P952LVU	ERF articulated
R281JMA	ERF articulated

This Proctor 4 wheeler FVJ836 was acquired with its 'A' licence in the mid-1950s and marked Harry Morgan's entry into steel haulage. The vehicle is shown being used as a float at Cwm Carnival.

This Bedford 'O' series 5 ton short wheelbase tipper DBK909 fitted with greedy boards was used to deliver miner's coal from local collieries.

Pictured at the rear of Ash Street, Cwm, this small 'A' series Bedford HUH222 was used on Harry Morgan's coal round.

This pair of BMC 7 ton flats, LKG533 and NBO89 were purchased new from City Motors, Cardiff. They were operated out of Richard Thomas & Baldwin's Ebbw Vale Steelworks and are shown at the rear of No. 12, Ash Street, Cwm, loaded with sheet steel.

This Albion 6 wheeler VVJ123 was one of two Reivers purchased together with their Licences from Parfitts of Ebbw Vale. The other vehicle was VVJ294. Both had originally been delivered to Parfitts by Praills of Hereford. In the background and barely visible is Harry Morgan's Thames Trader articulated unit coupled to a single axle semi-trailer. This is believed to be the first articulated outfit to regularly work out of Ebbw Vale works.

Photographed in 1964 outside Harry Morgan's Newcombe Tarrace premises at Cwm, are a Dodge 4 wl rigid flat 932HWO and a Dodge articulated tractor unit AAX67B.

When bought new in 1970 this Leyland Beaver tractor unit VWO634H was Harry Morgan's pride and joy. Operated for many years on long-distance work, the vehicle is still owned by the firm, although no longer in service.

Three views of the Cwm depot of H. Morgan & Sons Haulage Ltd., and its fleet of tractor units.

Top: In the late 1970s the fleet comprised a Leyland Beaver, two ERF 'B' series, an Atkinson Borderer and Daf 2300 and 2800s.

Centre: By the mid-1980s Daf 2800, Leyland, Leyland Daf, and Foden units were being operated.

Bottom: In the early 1990s ERF 'C' series, Leyland, Leyland Daf, and Foden units made up the fleet with a single Daf 2800 surviving.

Above: A pair of Leyland tractor units, C339KGT and F485OTC are flanked by a Daf 2800 and a Foden.

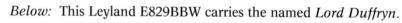

Below: This Leyland E829BBW carries the named *Lord Duffryn*.

In the 1980s secondhand purchases of Daf 2800 tractor units made up the backbone of the fleet.

Above: LUH493X dated from 1981

Below: B459ATH was from the 1984 era.

Opposite Top:
ERF – E806UKG carried the name *Duffryn Prince.*

Opposite bottom:
This ERF E101TDW was *Duffryn Princess.*

Above:
Duffryn Duke – E395SWD was an ERF 6x2 twin-steer tractor unit.

Right:
To mark the 50th Anniversary of H. Morgan & Sons fleet in 1995 an appropriate emblem was displayed on their vehicles.

Following de-nationalisation in the early 1950s Tim Price re-entered road transport with secondhand purchases together with their 'A' licences from British Road Services. His first new lorries coming in 1956 when he bought three Albion 4 wheel flats, PAX262, PAX263 and PAX264. In 1957 he bought his first new 8 wheelers, these being a pair of Leyland Octopus with double drive, RAX700 and RAX710. RAX710 is pictured new; note the tailboard, which was a feature in the fleet until the mid-1970s.

The composition of the Tim Price fleet changed dramatically following the closure of Pilkington's Glassworks at Pontypool. The entry into articulation came in that year with the purchase of a Leyland Marathon operating at 32 gross tons, and a year later with a number of Leyland Boxers grossing at 22 tons. These acquisitions were marred by the vehicles being unreliable in service, and they were soon replaced by secondhand purchases of Gardner 180 engined ERF and Atkinsons. Subsequently a number of new Maguris Deutz appeared in the late 1970s, but it was not long before the fleet was standardised on Mercedes.

Above:
One of the Maguris Deutz units purchased in the late 1970s.

Opposite top:
Mercedes tractor unit OWX992W seen in the Polo Grounds trailer park. Note the coil trailers in the background.

Opposite bottom:
OWX992W coupled to a van trailer.

Above:
A pair of Mercedes articulated tractor units, OWX994W and KHB237W shown coupled to van-bodied trailers.

Right:
Two of Tim Price's drivers, Messrs Jowitt and Childs with their vehicles at a Truck Rally.

F. PROSSER & SON, NEWPORT

Four generations of the Prosser family from Newport were involved with the movement of cattle and sheep. Originally they were drovers moving stock on foot from Newport to as far afield as Brecon. With the advent of the motor vehicle they entered haulage as livestock transporters, and became one of the main contractors in and around the Newport area. By the mid-1970s with the changing marketing techniques, which saw larger farms supplying direct to supermarket chains, and the reduction in local butchers shops, the fourth generation decided to call it a day and withdraw from the business.

Above:
The fleet of F. Prosser & Son at Lyne Road, Newport, in 1937 dressed up to celebrate the Coronation of King George VI. Pictured in front of the Commer stock lorries DW8884 and DW8144 are from left, driver Jim Sadler (Harry's son-in-law), owner Harry Prosser, drover Jack Rowlands, and son Ron Prosser.

Left:
Harry Prosser and son Ron seen loading sheep at Newport Cattle Market in the 1930s.

W.G. WATKINS & SONS, ABERGAVENNY

The history of W.G. Watkins and Sons of Triley Mill, Abergavenny, goes back over a century. Mainly involved as millers, they also had an involvement as hay and straw merchants. Not regarded as hauliers in the conventional sense, they nonetheless had hauled steel and other products not associated with their core activities.

A Leyland Boxer rigid 4 wheeler owned by W.G. Watkins & Son pauses in a familiar country scene in Monmouthshire.

Bedford TK – ONO358N is pictured at Triley Mill, near Abergavenny with a load of small hay bales.

Another view of ONO358N, but this time loaded with eighteen large round bales of straw.

Parked for the weekend at Triley Mill – Bedford TM JTX564W and Bedford TK, ONO358N.

Another small Bedford TK, but without an above cab extension, with a useful load of small bales of hay.

Bedford TM, JTX564W forms the backdrop for a business discussion.

J.M. WATKINS, ABERGAVENNY

John Mills Watkins who was born in 1907 was the son of a miller who ran the family business from Triley Mill, near Abergavenny. He initially worked for his father, and in 1937 started delivering sweets after his own days work was completed for the Uskvale Sweet Factory, Ross Road, Abergavenny. Thus his entry into haulage, albeit in a small way was accomplished with a small van, but by the war he owned a Thornycroft 4 wheeler which was employed on general haulage.

After the war he expanded further, using Atkinson 4 wheelers and 6 wheeled drawbar outfits, mainly carrying steel from Richard Thomas and Baldwin at Ebbw Vale, Whiteheads of Newport and Guest, Keen and Nettleford at Cardiff. He was soon obtaining regular back loads, the main customer being London Brick at Bedford.

In addition to haulage he also dealt in water turbines, generators and Lister diesel engines, and also operated a wholesale fruit and vegetable business. In addition if someone wanted to buy a lorry, he was the man to see.

His fleet of heavy vehicles was swallowed up in 1949 by nationalisation, but in 1953 he was back again operating by now mainly eight wheelers. When he first started in haulage he operated from the site of the family business at Triley Mill, later moving to Union Road, Abergavenny, thence from premises at the rear of the Boucher's Garage in Merthyr Road, Abergavenny to premises at the top of Belmont Road. During this period many of the vehicles were parked overnight and at weekends in the Fairfield at Abergavenny. In 1968 he decided to obtain premises on one site, and in that year built a purpose-built garage at Llanfoist on the outskirts of Abergavenny with direct access to the Heads of the Valleys Road. These premises were appropriately named 'Westgate Garage'.

In 1966 he was joined in the business by his son John, who became involved mainly in the maintenance of the rapidly expanding fleet.

Although Leyland, AEC, ERF and Foden 8 wheelers had been used, and they had bought their first articulated outfits in 1964 from Dodge, the father and son decided to standardise on ERF, which they considered came out on top in price, spare part availability and running costs. Thus from 1966, apart from a brief trial with a Volvo F86 in 1968, the fleet was entirely of ERF manufacture. Gardner engines were originally favoured – 150, 180 and finally 240, but with the advent of the motorway network the transition was made to Cummins engined vehicles.

With his father's death John continued to operate a substantial fleet, but he anticipated the contraction of industry with falling freight rates in actual terms and expanding fleets, and decided it was time to finish. Thus J.M. Watkins a substantial Abergavenny transport business disappeared.

Above:
Photographed at Abergavenny Carnival in the late 1940s just prior to nationalisation are two Atkinsons. On the left a 6 wheeler, Fleet No: 12 with a 4 wheeler HNY794 (10). Shown with the vehicles are Wilf Williams, Mike Bevan and John Davies (who spent 25 years driving for J.M. Watkins).

Opposite top:
The chains securing this load of steel pipes parted at the approach to a roundabout, resulting in the top part of the cab of ERF AAX153K being crushed. Fortunately the driver survived, fracturing his arm.

Opposite bottom:
J.M. Watkins maintained and hauled trailers for the New North Road Federation, carrying racing pigeons to all parts of the country. This dramatic view shows thousands of pigeons being let loose at the start of a race at Carlisle. The leading vehicle is Watkins' ERF YUH902T fitted with a Gardner 8LXB (240) engine, which entered the fleet new in 1979. It was driven by Tim Barry who drove for the firm for around 18 years.

Above:
A line of sixteen ERF tractor units at J.M. Watkins' premises at Westgate Garage, Llanfoist, Abergavenny in 1974.

Opposite top:
This ERF 'E' series tractor unit, D719MKG dating from 1987 was fitted with a 320 Cummins engine, and is shown coupled to an extendable trailer laden with steelwork which was hauled from Watsons of Bristol to the site of the World Trade Centre at Churchill Way, Cardiff.

Opposite bottom:
This 100 year old pleasure boat was carried from Worcester to French Bros. Runnymede Boatyard using ERF, D719MKG with its trailer extended from 40ft to 60ft.

This Leyland Octopus 8 wheeler KWN493 loaded with bagged sugar caught fire, and although severely damaged was repaired and put back into service. This was one of a number of vehicles bought together with their 'A' Carrier's Licence from British Road Services, following de-nationalisation.

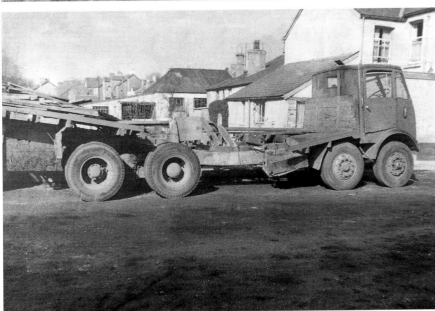

Left:
Operated internally at Ebbw Vale Steelworks, the career of this Atkinson 8 wheeler came to a sudden end when a steel coil was accidentally dropped from a great height.

Cyril Williams operated ten eight wheelers in Ebbw Vale Works internally on scrap. This contract operated 24 hours a day, 365 days of the year. This AEC Mammoth Major Mk5 had been driven over the bank by a trespasser into the works.

Top left: This non-standard Dennis 8 wheeler OPD56 was an unusual vehicle. Cyril Williams had a number of these special conversions in his fleet.

Top right: Seen loading in Ebbw Vale works this Thornycroft Trusty 8 wheeler HEU686 was one of the last of its type produced by this manufacturer.

Above left: This Leyland Octopus 8 wheeler PDG392 was on contract to Richard Thomas & Baldwin and was painted in their own livery, which by now was light blue with black lettering.

Above right: This Atkinson tractor unit BEU385D was fitted with a Gardner 6LX (150) engine and was driven by Gareth Thomas. Articulation started to appear in the Cyril Williams fleet from 1964.

Left: An Austin 4 wl flat HEU892.

Brynmawr, where Cyril Williams was based, was originally in Breconshire. Local Government re-organisation in 1974 brought the town into the County of Gwent. It is a fact that when it snows in Gwent, blizzards come down in Brynmawr, and traffic grinds to a halt there before anywhere else. This is evidenced by these views of an Albion 4 wheeler KEU892 being dug out.

Left:
Cyril Williams takes delivery of a new Bedford from Atlas Garages, Newport.

Below:
With the contraction of the steel industry in South Wales Cyril Williams set about diversifying his fleet. As a result he was responsible for the distribution of Crompton Electric Vehicles throughout the United Kingdom and Eire. For this purpose he found the Foden tractor unit with a Gardner 180 engine particularly suitable. This view shows Foden LEU625K so employed.

Above: Foden MEU266L is loaded with four electric tugs.

Below: This Foden LEU460K is taking part in a local carnival.

This Scammel Contractor 240 ton drawbar tractor, YWO24T (633) is on display at Astle Park, Cheshire, in August 2001. Named *Musketeer*, it was new to Robert Wynn & Sons Ltd., Newport in 1979. It is now preserved by Graham Booth of Southport.

Diamond 'T' PDW321 (266) was originally registered to Robert Wynn & Sons (Manchester) Ltd in June, 1958. It is shown at a breakers yard, but is now happily in preservation.

Graham Booth's preserved Scammell Contractor KAX395P (600) at Stoneleigh, Worcestershire in August, 2002. YWO24T is in the background.

This Foden 6wl. 60 ton drawbar tractor which was acquired new in July, 1942 formed the backbone of the WYNNS heavy haulage fleet during and in the immediate post-war period. Shown at both ends of its career, it is (above) operating in the Second World War, and (below) as a wrecker on trade plates in the late 1950s.

Wynns acquired eleven of these FWD Su-Coe timber tractors from the War Department following the Second World War. This vehicle FDW79 (79) entered service in May, 1950. The firm had a depot for the timber side of the business at Welshpool in Mid-Wales.

Scammell Pioneer DDW495 (140) was one of the two ex-WD tank transporters operated by WYNNS. This example entered their service in August, 1946.

Photographed new in 1958 by Scammell Lorries Ltd., Watford, this Scammell Highwayman articulated tractor unit was delivered to E.B. Rees Ltd., of Usk, Monmouthshire, and registered as TAX352. They normally operated the vehicle on steel traffic in their green livery, but in 1960 it passed to Parfitt of Ebbw Vale and for a short period operated out of Ebbw Vale Steelworks in maroon paintwork.

Acquired in that same year by Robert Wynn & Sons Ltd., Newport, the vehicle was mainly used by them as a tar tanker out of Nantgarw. In April, 1967 it was sold to Logan of Penperlleni (Goytre) who converted it into a ballasted breakdown truck, and again in maroon livery. Later in its career it was repainted yellow, more suited to its breakdown and recovery role. It survives today as a prized possession of the Logan family.

P.M. HEATON PUBLISHING

Paul Heaton was born at New Inn, Pontypool, in 1944 and was educated at Greenlawn Junior School in New Inn and the Wern Secondary School at Sebastopol. At fifteen he commenced employment, at first in a local store and then with a builders' merchant. A year later he was appointed as a Deck Cadet in the Merchant Navy, with the Lamport & Holt Line of Liverpool, and served in their vessels *Chatham, Constable* and *Romney* usually in the Brazil and River Plates trades. he joined the Monmouthshire Constabulary (now Gwent) in 1963, and served at Abergavenny, Cwmbran, Newport, the Traffic Department, the Motor Cycle Section, as the Press Liaison Officer, and for five years represented Inspectors for the whole of Wales nationally on the Joint Central Committee of the Police Federation. he was promoted to sergeant in 1974 and Inspector in 1982. On his retirement he served as Market Inspector with the RSPCA for eight years and at the same time was Landlord of a Public House for three years.

He has always maintained an interest in maritime history and in transport generally, and for a period of ten years had numerous articles published in the magazine *Sea Breezes*. He has had the following books published:

Reardon Smith 1905-1980 (1980)
The Baron Glanely of St. Fagans and W.J. Tatem Ltd., with H.S. Appleyard (1980)
The 'Redbrook', A Deep-Sea Tramp (1981) four editions
The 'Usk' Ships (1982) two editions
The Abbey Line (1983)
Kaye, Son & Co. Ltd., with K. O'Donoghue (1983)
Reardon Smith Line (1984) two editions
The South American Saint Line (1985)
Welsh Blockade Runners in the Spanish Civil War (1985)
Lamport & Holt (1986) two editions
Tatems of Cardiff (1987)
Booth Line (1987)
Jack Billmeir, Merchant Shipowner (1989)
Welsh Shipping, Forgotten Fleets (1989)
The Gallant Ship 'Stephen Hopkins' , with R.J. Witt (1990)
Palm Line, with Laurence Dunn (1994)
Not All Coppers Are ...! (1994)
Wynns – The First 100 Years for John Wynn (1995) three editions
Wynns – The Last 20 Years for John Wynn (1996)
L.C. Lewis, Heavy Haulage (1996)
Wynns Overseas first draft for John Wynn (1998)
Lamport & Holt Line (2004)
The Wynns Fleet - 120 Years of Road Haulage (2003)
Road Transport Gwent (2004)